# GOLDEN RETRIEVER

## THE BREED STANDARD ILLUSTRATED

**Wendy Andrews**

Published by Catcombe Publications,
Catcombe, Hilmarton, Calne,
Wiltshire SN11 9HR. England.

Printed by J. W. Arrowsmith Ltd.,
Bristol, England.

Second Edition

Copyright © Wendy Andrews 1999

All rights reserved. No part of this book may be reproduced or utilized in any form or by any means, electronic or mechanical including photocopying, recording or by any information storage and retrieval system, without permission in writing from the author.

This publication is sold subject to the conditions that it shall not, by way of trade or otherwise, be lent, resold, hired out, or otherwise circulated without the author's prior consent in any form of binding or cover other than that in which it is published and without similar conditions including this condition being imposed upon any subsequent purchaser.

British Library Cataloguing-in-Publication Data
A catalogue record for this book is available from the British Library

ISBN 0 9536245 0 1

Cover Photographs of
**Champion Millgreen Magnum** 11C.C.s, 10 B.O.B.s
Sh Ch Tokeida Starstealer x Catcombe Cher at Millgreen C.C. & Res C.C.

# Introduction

This book was complited in response to my being invited to speak on Conformation, Terminology and Movement at two Breed Seminars hosted by The Southern Golden Retriever Club and The South Western Golden Retriever Club respectively.
For the seminars, I decided that a visual, using drawings and diagrams, rather than an purely oral approach, would be a clearer and more easily understood way of explaining the points made within the Breed Standard. This book is based on the drawings I produced.

# Acknowledgements

My sincere thanks go to my family for their support, to Fiona Joint who has given me much encouragement and help with proof reading the script. Thanks to Brian and Monica Booth for help with the photographs used within the book, to Fergus Durr for the photograph used on the front cover, and to David Dalton for the photograph used on the back cover.

# *Foreword*

I consider it to be a great privilege and, indeed, honour to be asked by Wendy Andrews to write the 'Foreword' for this quite remarkable work. The clarity, detailed portrayal and analysis of the breed standard is exceptionally high; to a degree that it immediately elevates it into the realm of a classic.

The blurb, as given on the back cover, emphasises from the start the fact that a Golden Retriever is first and foremost a gundog, a retriever - that is what it was designed to be. I use the word *design* purposefully, for the breed standard skeletal structure was evolved to produce a dog that could traverse rough country with the greatest possible ease and speed, which could be achieved through constructive breeding.

Quite recently I was with a friend of many years standing, who hunted foxhounds for some thirty five years. Having already talked to Wendy about this book I put a question to him. "When you get puppies back to kennels, after being at walk, what is the first thing you look for?" (For those who don't know, hound puppies are reared by hunt supporters, this is known as 'walking' and returned to kennels when fully grown). Without a seconds hesitation he replied, "Shoulders of course. A straight shouldered hound has to take four, maybe five, strides to keep up with a hound with a correctly angulated shoulder that is covering the same amount of ground in three. So, in a long hunt the former frequently tail off."

Exactly the same applies to a working gundog. Equally important are the hindquarters, the powerhouse of any quadruped. The hocks should be well let down, vertical to the ground when viewed from the side and straight when viewed from behind, with good angulation to the stifle, providing the power and drive required. Regretably these days one sees dogs high in the awards at shows with varying degrees of sickle and cow hocks. Shoulders, too, frequently leave much to be desired.

Wendy covers every factor that must be taken into considerstion in attempting to produce the faultless Golden Retriever, were such a dog, indeed any such animal possible, but all the avenues are covered in this most versatile, comprehensive and clearly illustrated book, delineating the correct from the incorrect throughout the entire breed standard.

Not satisfied with this achievement, she has added *icing to the cake* by the inclusion of quite remarkable photographs defining the permisable range of colour and correctness of coat.

This book is a MUST for those who are seriously considering breeding, judging in the future, or, indeed, have already started out along the latter road; further it could provide a timely and informative refresher of the breed standard for all judges. I had my first Golden in 1946; I have no hesitation in saying that, since then, this is by far the most explicit and helpful work on the conformation of the Golden Retriever I have encountered and it will certainly be added to my library.

Michael F. Twist.   23/12/1999

# Contents

| Subject | Page No |
|---|---|
| Foreword | 4 |
| Points of the Golden Retriever | 6 - 7 |
| The Skeleton of the Golden Retriever | 8 - 9 |
| Muscle Structure | 10 - 11 |
| The Standard of the Breed | 12 - 13 |
| Understanding the Breed Standard | 14 |
| The Golden Retriever as a Gundog | 15 |
| General Appearance | 16 - 17 |
| Characteristics | 18 - 19 |
| Temperament | 20 - 21 |
| Head and Skull, Eyes and Ears | 22 - 25 |
| The Mouth and Teeth | 26 - 29 |
| The Neck | 30 - 31 |
| Forequarters - Seen from the Front | 32 - 35 |
| Shoulder Angulation | 36 - 39 |
| The Body - The Spine and Rib Cage | 40 - 45 |
| The Body - The Loin and Coupling | 46 - 47 |
| The Topline | 48 - 51 |
| Tail Carriage | 52 - 53 |
| Tail Set | 54 - 55 |
| Hindquarters - See from the Rear | 56 - 59 |
| Pelvis and Croup | 60 - 61 |
| Stifle Angulation | 62 - 63 |
| The Hocks | 64 - 65 |
| Feet | 66 |
| Pasterns | 67 |
| Size - Height and Weight | 68 - 69 |
| Faults | 70 - 71 |
| The Coat | 72 - 75 |
| Colour | 76 - 77 |
| Movement - Line of Convergence | 78 - 79 |
| Movement - Single Tracking | 80 |
| Movement - Rear | 81 |
| Movement - Front | 82 - 83 |
| Movement - Side | 84 - 85 |
| Anatomical Systems involved with Movement | 86 - 89 |
| Development of the Breed Standard | 90 - 93 |
| American Standard of the Golden Retriever | 94 - 96 |
| Terminology | 97 - 99 |
| Index | 100 |

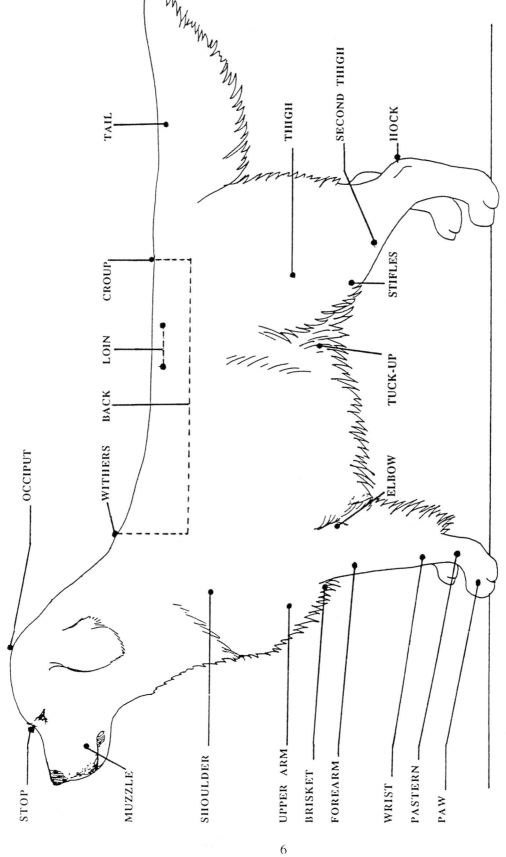

# Points of the Dog

| | |
|---|---|
| **Occiput** | Upper back part of skull. |
| **Elbow** | The joint between the upper arm and the forearm. |
| **Withers** | The highest point of the body, immediately behind the neck. The height of the dog is measured from this point to the ground. |
| **Stop** | The point of the face where the end of the muzzle steps up to the skull. Indentation between the eyes where the nasal bone and the skull meet. |
| **Forearm** | The bone of the forelegs between the elbow and wrist. |
| **Back** | Generally it is the top line of the dog between the two points of withers and croup, however some standards state that it is the region between withers and loin. |
| **Hock** | The tarsus joint on the hind leg between the bottom of the second thigh and the metatarsus. |
| **Wrist** | Is made up of the carpal bones and it lies above the front pastern. |
| **Loin** | The part of the body between the last rib and the pelvis. Can also be referred to as the 'girth' or 'waist'. |
| **Thigh** | The part of the hindquarter from the hip to the stifle. |
| **Pastern** | The region of the foreleg between the carpus (wrist) and the digits (toes). |
| **Shoulder** | The blade in the forequarters of the dog of which the bottom part meets the top of the humerus and the top part lies just behind the neck. |
| **Second thigh** | In the hindquarters, it is the lower thigh from the stifle to the hock. |
| **Croup** | On the back, between the front of the pelvis and the root of the tail. |
| **Brisket** | The forepart of the body below the chest and between the forelegs. |
| **Stifle** | The point where the thigh and second thigh meet in the hindquarters. The knee joint. |
| **Upper Arm** | Is the humerus of the foreleg running from the base of the scapula to the elbow joint. |
| **Tuck - Up** | The concave underline of the body that curves upwards from the end of the ribs to the waist. |

# The Skeleton
## of the
## Golden Retriever

# Skeleton of the Golden Retriever

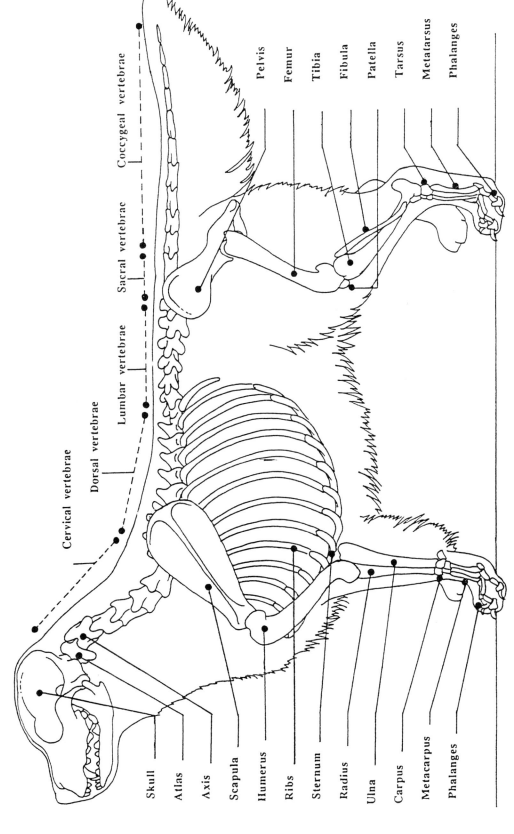

# The Muscles
## of the
## Golden Retriever

# Muscles of the Golden Retriever

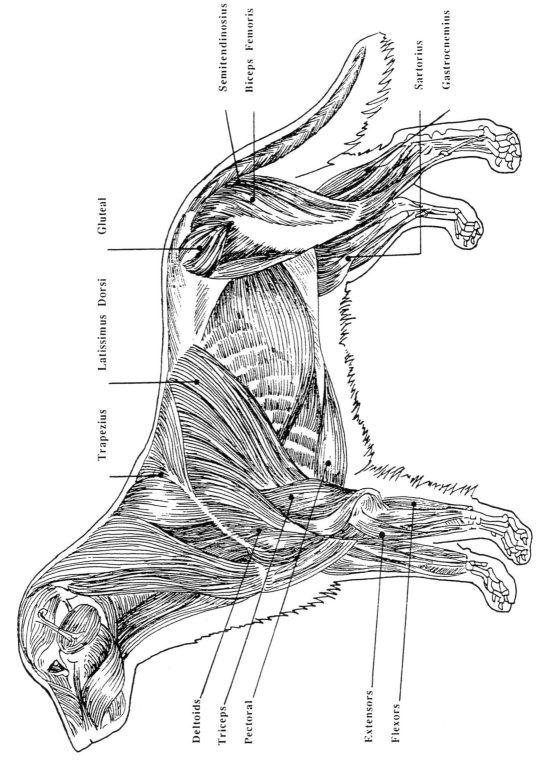

# The Golden Retriever
# BREED STANDARD
*Kennel Club of Great Britain*

| | |
|---|---|
| **General Appearance** | Symmetrical, balanced, active, powerful, level mover, sound, with kindly expression. |
| **Characteristics** | Biddable, intelligent and possessing natural working ability. |
| **Temperament** | Kindly, friendly and confident. |
| **Head and Skull** | Balanced and well-chiselled, skull broad without coarseness; well set on neck, muzzle powerful, wide and deep. Length of foreface approximately equals length from well-defined stop to occiput. Nose preferably black. |
| **Eyes** | Dark brown, set well apart, dark rims. |
| **Ears** | Moderate size, set on approximate level with eyes. |
| **Mouth** | Jaws strong, with a perfect, regular and complete scissor bite, i.e. Upper teeth closely overlapping lower teeth and set to the jaws. |
| **Neck** | Good length, clean and muscular. |
| **Forequarters** | Forelegs straight with good bone, shoulders well laid back, long in blade with upper arm of equal length placing legs well under body. Elbows close fitting. |
| **Body** | Balanced, short coupled, deep through heart. Ribs deep and well sprung. Level topline. |

# The Golden Retreiver
# BREED STANDARD
*Kennel Club of Great Britain*

| | |
|---|---|
| ***Hindquarters*** | Loin and legs strong and muscular, good second thighs, well bent stifles. Hocks well let down, straight when viewed from rear, neither turning in nor out. Cowhocks highly undesirable. |
| ***Feet*** | Round and cat-like. |
| ***Tail*** | Set on and carried level with back, reaching the hocks, without curl at tip. |
| ***Gait/Movement*** | Powerful with good drive. Straight and true in front and rear. Stride long and free with no sign of hackney action in front. |
| ***Coat*** | Flat or wavy with good feathering, dense water-resisting undercoat. |
| ***Colour*** | Any shade of gold or cream, neither red nor mahogany. A few white hairs on chest only, permissible. |
| ***Size*** | Height at withers: Dogs 56-61 cms (22-24 ins), Bitches 51-56 cms (20-22 ins). |
| ***Faults*** | Any departure from the foregoing points should be considered a fault and the seriousness with which the fault should be regarded should be in exact proportion to its degree. |
| Note | Male animals should have two apparently normal testicles fully descended into the scrotum. |

# Understanding the Breed Standard

### The Breed Standard is the blueprint of the ideal Golden Retriever.

The Standard is a written specification of the attributes needed in a perfect Golden Retriever. Words are used to descibe a visual image, and since individual people perceive things slightly differently their interpretations of the Standard will vary. What might be the 'ideal' dog for one person, could be faulted by another.

The quest for perfection should be every breeders aim. But whether one is a breeder, exhibiter or judge, it is important that we analyse and understand the Breed Standard more fully.

# The Golden Retriever is a Gundog

## One should never forget this.

First and foremost, the Golden Retriever was developed and bred to collect dead and wounded game in the shooting field and the Standard clearly reflects the requirements of the breed as a working gundog .

The Breed Standard
# *General Appearance*

- *Symmetrical, balanced*
- *Active, powerful, level mover*
- *Sound*
- *With kindly expression*

# First Impressions

The Breed Standard begins by giving a summary of the 'essence' of the Golden Retriever. The qualities that give 'Breed character', distinguishing it from other breeds. Essential components are his overall appearance of an active, powerful, sound dog, being well proportioned and balanced, and with a temperament that is kindly and biddable. Originally intended as a retriever of game birds, he is a dog of some speed and considerable endurance, capable of working in all weathers and conditions, and so should be shown in hard muscular condition.

# Symmetry and Balance

**Balanced and symmetrical.** A balanced appearance is hard to define but is instantly recognizable and so is its absence! No exaggerations, no extremes and every part in proportion, one to the other.

Symmetrical does not mean square! The dictionary defines it as *"the proportion between parts, balance of arrangement between two sides. Order, shapliness and harmony."*

**The overall proportion of the balanced Golden Retriever is of a dog a little longer than he is tall. The length of leg should be half of the height.** Measured from the withers to the elbow and from the elbow to the ground. (see Diagram A.)

Below are examples of different height to length ratios - length of back and length of leg - and how exaggerations of either unbalance the overall proportions of the dog.

### A   Correct
Outline of Champion Styal Scott of Glengilde (the Record holder of Challenge Certificates for the Breed). A classic example of correct balance and symmetry.

### B   Incorrect
The length of back has been increased by 10% This makes the body far too long and the legs appear to be too short by comparison.

### C   Incorrect
The length of leg has been increased by 10% making the dog unbalanced and high on the leg.

The Breed Standard
# *Characteristics*

* *Biddable*

* *Intelligent*

* *Possessing natural working ability*

# *Biddability*

## *The desire to please.*

Golden Retrievers generally have this in abundance. It is one of their most endearing features. Working with and for people have made them a popular choice not only as working gundogs, but as guide dogs, hearing dogs, dogs for the disabled and also as willing partners in organised events such as obedience, agility, conformation shows etc., as well as their unsurpassed and ever popular role as trusted family companions.

Biddability, intelligence and natural working ability are characteristics that are undoubtedly most desirable in the complete dog, but for the purpose of assessing a Golden Retriever against this standard in the ring, it is not feasible to evaluate these particular qualites with any certainty.

## **Intelligent and possessing natural working ability.**

***Active, powerful and sound....*** and able to carry a heavy bird over rough plough or jump with a hare over obstacles or swim through floodwater with a duck...and to work all day.

The Breed Standard
# *Temperament*

* *Kindly*

* *Friendly*

* *Confident*

# Temperament
## Kindly, friendly and confident.

The trustworthy, and affectionate nature of the Golden Retriever is his most important asset. It comes before any physical attribute. Breeders must always ensure that, in their breeding programmes, temperament is their number one priority.

*'Kindly'* is mentioned twice in the Standard. First *'kindly expression'* then again here together with *'friendly and confident.'*. These qualities do shine forth and can be considered when judging, and particularly so if the dog exhibits the reverse!

The dog that shows any type of aggression or hostility without provocation can not be accepted as typical of the breed.

The Breed Standard
# Head and Skull

* Balanced and well-chiselled

* Skull broad without coarseness

* Well set on neck

* Muzzle powerful, wide and deep

* Length of foreface approximately equals length from well-defined stop to occiput

* Nose preferably black

# Eyes

* Dark brown, set well apart, dark rims

# Ears

* Moderate size, set on approximate level with eyes

# Heads

***Balanced and well-chiselled heads with kindly expressions.***

It is difficult to define in words what makes an excellent head different from an ordinary head. Very small changes in proportion, shape and planes alter the balance and expression.

With heads, even though we have the Breed Standard firmly in mind, we all have differing and subjective interpretations of the ideal - what may be admired by one person could, at the same time, be faulted by another.

***It is impossible to illustrate one single head that would appeal equally to everyone!***

# Heads
## Proportion and shape of Skull and Muzzle

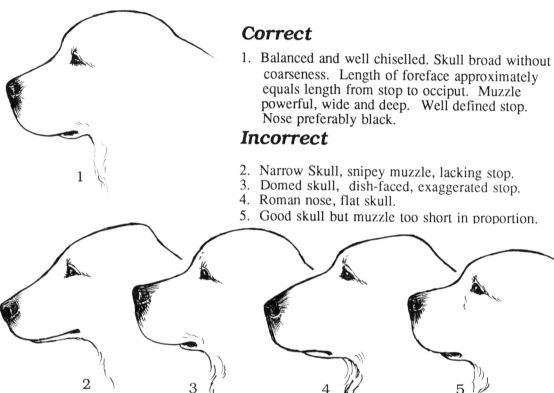

### Correct

1. Balanced and well chiselled. Skull broad without coarseness. Length of foreface approximately equals length from stop to occiput. Muzzle powerful, wide and deep. Well defined stop. Nose preferably black.

### Incorrect

2. Narrow Skull, snipey muzzle, lacking stop.
3. Domed skull, dish-faced, exaggerated stop.
4. Roman nose, flat skull.
5. Good skull but muzzle too short in proportion.

# Eyes

**Correct**
Correct shape. Dark brown set well apart with dark rims. Kindly expression.

**Incorrect**
Too large and round. Too black giving a glaring untypical expression.

**Incorrect**
Slanting triangular shape. Iris too light, giving hard expression. Light eye rims.

# Heads - Ears & Ear Carriage

**Correct**
In repose.

**Correct**
At attention.

**Incorrect**
Too large.

**Incorrect**
Too low set and houndy

**Incorrect**
Too high set.

**Incorrect**
Too small and 'flyaway'

**Heads - Sex differences**

You should be able to tell the sex of a Retriever from its head. A bitch should have a head which is distinctly feminine, but not weak. The head of a male should be more masculine, impressive and larger (in proportion to his larger size). A bitch with a strong 'doggy' head or a dog with a 'bitchy' head to be faulted.

The Breed Standard
# *The Mouth*

* *Jaws strong with*

* *Perfect, regular and complete scissor bite
i.e. Upper teeth closely overlapping lower teeth and set to the jaws*

# The Skull and Teeth

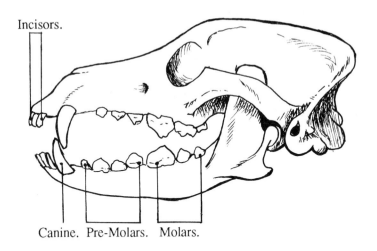

## The Teeth

**Canine**..................................................Riping and Puncturing
**Incisors**..................................................Slicing
**Pre-Molars**..............................................Gripping
**Molars**..................................................Grinding

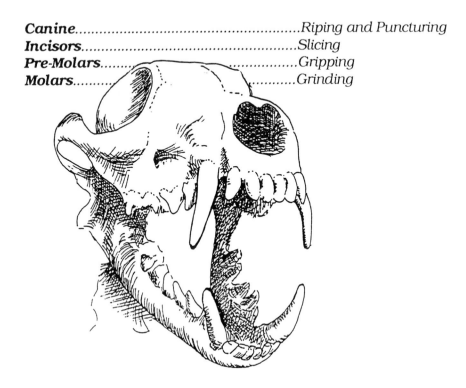

# The Mouth

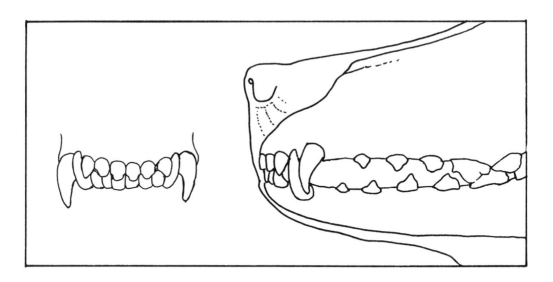

## The Correct Scissor Bite

Desired as the strongest and least wearing.

The inner surface of the upper incisors contact the outer surfaces of the lower ones.

The small pre-molars do not touch. This is carrying space. They are set in a "saw tooth" pattern with the points of the upper set into the gaps of the lower. This is efficient for gripping

The upper molars closely overlap the lower in a shearing action.

# The Mouth  Incorrect Bites

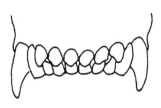 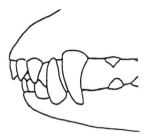

**Overshot**  The incisors of the upper jaw overlap but fail to contact the incisors of the lower jaw.

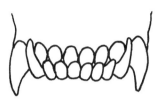 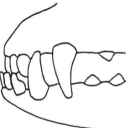

**Undershot**  The extra length of the lower jaw causes the incisors to project out beyond the incisors of the upper jaw.

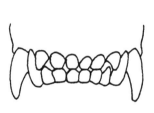 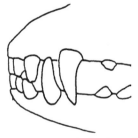

**Level or Pincer Bite**  The edge to edge meeting of the incisors is wearing

 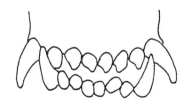

**Misalignment of Teeth**
Central incisors are out of line and forward of the rest. This in itself does not contitute an overshot bite.

**Wry Mouth with misplaced Teeth.**
The jaw is twisted and the teeth are badly misaligned.

The Breed Standard
# The Neck

* *Well set on neck*
* *Good length*
* *Clean and muscular*

# The Neck

### Correct
Neck of good length (reach)
Clean with no throatiness.
Strong and muscular.
The neckline 'flows' into
the shoulder.

### Incorrect
Lacking in muscular tone.
Neck is not 'well set on' as
the line is too angular and
does not flow into shoulders.

### Incorrect
A 'stuffy' neck.
Too short in length.
Throatiness under the jowl.
Shoulders loaded and
carrying too much weight.

The Breed Standard
# *Forequarters*

* *Forelegs straight with good bone*

* *Shoulders well laid back*

* *Shoulders long in blade with upper arm of equal length placing legs well under body*

* *Elbows close fitting*

# The Front

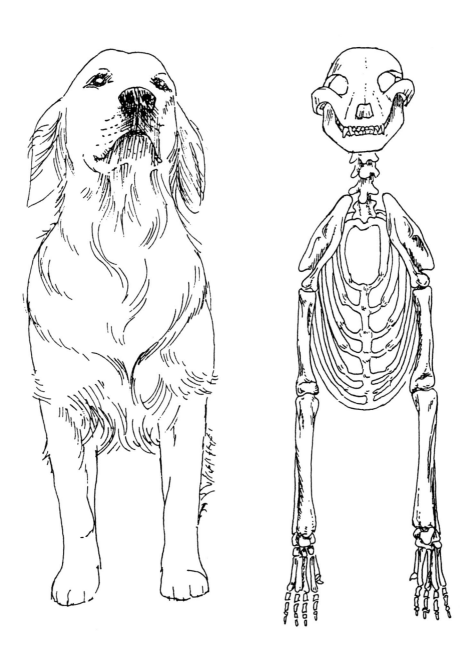

The Breed Standard
# Forequarters

* *Forelegs straight with good bone*

* *Elbows close fitting*

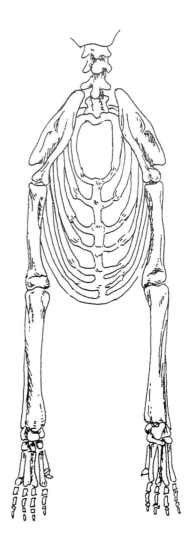

## Correct

**BONES STRAIGHT**

There is a straight line from the shoulder to the foot. This pillar of bones is both the strongest and most efficient for weight bearing and movement.

**The feet** are straight.
This is **correct**.

# The Front

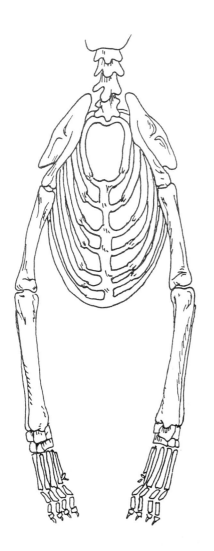 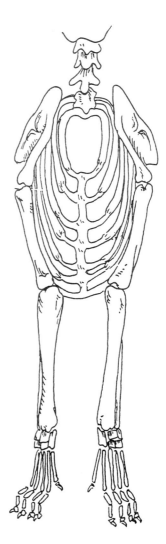

## Incorrect
**OUT AT ELBOW**

The elbows are not lying close to the rib cage, but are pushed outwards, breaking the straight line from shoulder to foot pad.

**The feet** are turned inwards. This is also **incorrect**.

## Incorrect
**IN AT ELBOW**

The elbows are pinched too close together under the rib cage. This breaks the straight line from shoulder to foot pad.

**The feet** are turned outwards. This is also **incorrect**.

The Breed Standard
# Forequarters

*   *Shoulders well laid back*

*   *Shoulders long in blade with upper arm of equal length placing legs well under body*

# Layback of Shoulder

The Standard does not specifically mention any degree of angles, but it is generally accepted that the term 'Well-laid shoulders', refers to the front assembly that has the scapula inclined at an angle of 45 degrees from the vertical.

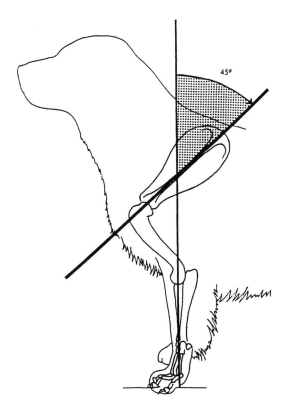

**A well laid shoulder inclined at 45° from the vertical**

## How do you measure?

It is one thing to study a paper diagram of a dog with the hair removed and the bones clearly defined; with lines superimposed and angles mathematically measured, and quite another to assess the live specimen where you only have your eyes to see and hands to FEEL what is not always clearly visible because of excess hair and muscle or fat. Added to that, as you *feel* the dog, you are standing partly over it, so you will have a changing viewpoint from the side to above, which needs to be taken into account.

In addition, it is not only the layback of the shoulder blade that you have to assess, but also the length of the humerus (upper arm) by comparison to the length of the scapula (shoulder blade), and the angle that they form.

*Feel* for the prominent part of the bones - the top of the shoulder blade at the withers; the shoulder joint in the front of the chest and the elbow joint. Use them as landmarks.

# Shoulder Angulation

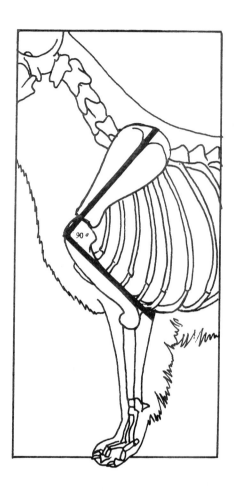

*Correct*

**IDEAL FRONT ASSEMBLY**

Showing the 45° layback of the shoulder blade - Scapula - and its 90° angle with the humerus.

The length of blade and upper arm should be more or less equal.

This enables the legs to be placed well under the body.

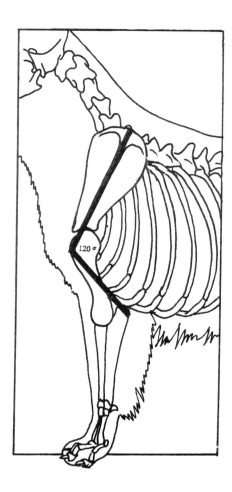

*Incorrect*

**POORLY ANGULATED FRONT**

Scapula (shoulder blade) and Humerus (upper arm) are too short. This opens up the obtuse angle between the two of them.

Note the legs are well forward and there is little forechest.

This is an upright shoulder.

# Shoulder Angulation

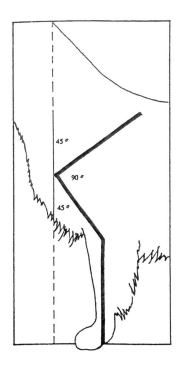

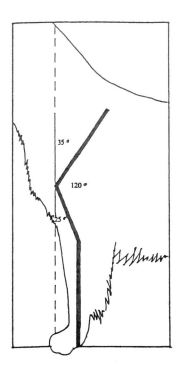

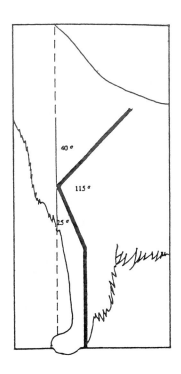

## Correct

### IDEAL FRONT

45° layback of the shoulder blade from the vertical and its 90° angle with the upper arm.

This assembly allows for greatest length of reach in movement, and with slightly sloping pasterns, greatest shock absorbency.

With the point of support, the foot pads, directly beneath the scapula, this front is well balanced.

## Incorrect

### POORLY ANGULATED

The shortness in length of the shoulder blades forces them far apart at the withers, thus weakening the structure.
With a poorly angulated front the length and reach of stride is limited, affecting movement.

There is less efficiency in shock absorbing, too.

Note the lack of forechest.

## Incorrect

### TERRIER FRONT

The shoulder blade is a fair length and well laid back but the upper arm is much too vertical.

The dog may have to lift his feet quite high in order to get sufficient length of stride. An exaggerated action and wasted energy!

Note the lack of forechest.

The Breed Standard
# The Body

* *Balanced*
* *Short coupled*
* *Deep through heart*
* *Ribs deep and well sprung*
* *Level topline*

# The Spine and Rib Cage

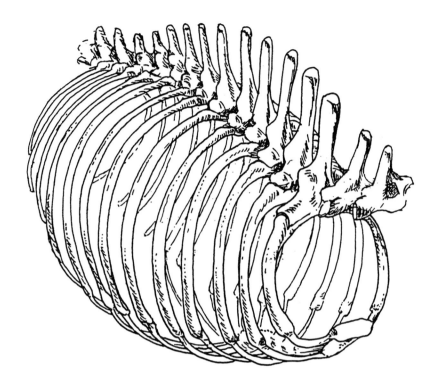

## The Rib Cage

The rib cage protects the heart and the lungs and is composed of thirteen pairs of ribs joined to the vertebrae. Nine pairs are attached to the sternum or breast bone and are called true ribs. The four pairs which are not attached to the sternum are called false or floating ribs.

The chest area enclosed by the ribcage must be capacious enough to allow maximum volume for the heart and lungs. This will provide buoyancy and stability in swimming.

The ribs should be arched out from the vertebrae and then drop to a deep oval to facilitate the smooth action of the forelimbs alongside the ribcage. This shape allows for the expansion and deflation of the chest during exertion.

## The Spine

The vertebra which contains the spinal cord comprises of seven cervical vertebrae or neck bones, thirteen dorsal vertebrae, seven lumbar vertebrae and three sacral vertebrae. The coccygeal vertebrae or tail bones vary in number according to the breed.

# The Rib Cage *Viewed from the front*

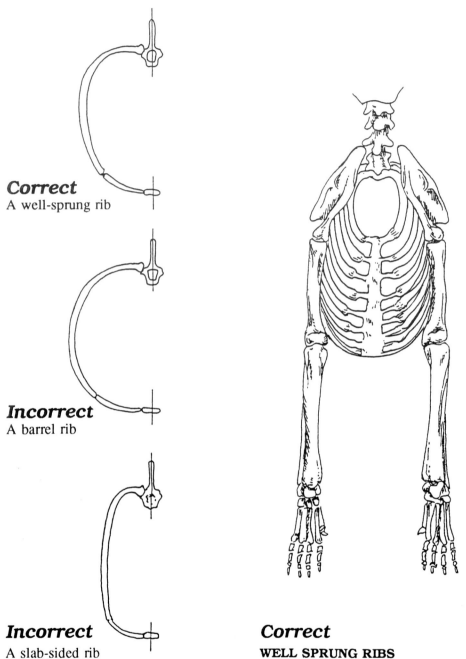

**Correct**
A well-sprung rib

**Incorrect**
A barrel rib

**Incorrect**
A slab-sided rib

**Correct**
**WELL SPRUNG RIBS**

There is plenty of room for lungs and heart. The oval shape allows for ease of movement of the forelimbs alongside chest wall.

# The Rib Cage *Viewed from the front*

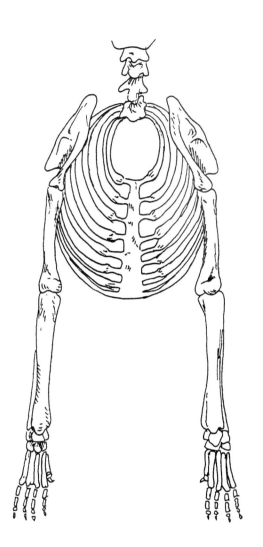
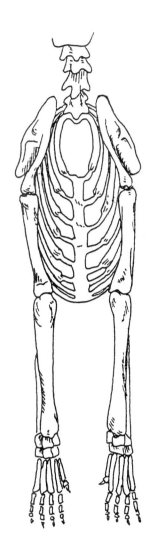

## Incorrect
**BARREL RIBS**

Chest far too wide, forcing the shoulder blades apart at the withers and making for awkward rolling front action.

## Incorrect
**SLAB-SIDED RIBS**

Chest far too narrow, with elbows too close together. Restricted lung and heart capacity. Lack of bouyancy in water.

The Breed Standard
# The Body

* *Deep through heart*
* *Ribs deep and well sprung*

# The Body
## The Shape of the Ribs & Undercarriage

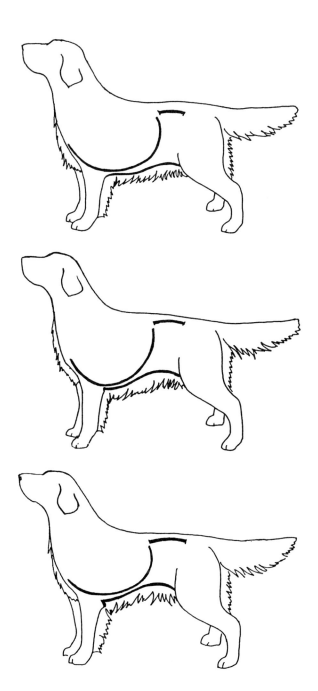

### Correct

**THIS RIB CAGE IS DEEP AND LONG**

It has depth at brisket, a good forechest, and the ribs are carried well-back. Good internal capacity for heart and lungs.

The abdomen is deep and firmly muscled, with a slight tuck-up.

### Incorrect

**THIS RIB CAGE IS LACKING IN DEPTH AT THE LAST RIBS.**

This restricts the internal capacity, even though it has adequate depth at the elbow.

This lack of depth is sometimes referred to as 'Herring Gutted'.

The flank is too 'cut-up', giving a rangey look.

### Incorrect

**THIS RIB CAGE IS TOO SHALLOW**

Lacking in depth (notice the elbows clearly visible). Very restricted lung capacity.

Lacking in development throughout, with very 'tucked-up' undercarriage.

The Breed Standard
# The Body

* **Balanced**
* **Short coupled**

# The Loin - The Coupling
## The Loin joins the front and rear assemblies

The Loin is a well muscled spinal 'bridge' behind the last rib and before the hip joint. Depending on its length, the dog is said to be long or short coupled. A long weak loin is obviously faulty. Too short could result in a lack of flexability.

**The length of the back and the shape of the rib cage affect the length of loin.**

## Correct

**SHORT COUPLED** with correct length of back (being in proportion to the dogs height).

Rib Cage deep and long.

**Short in loin** and therefore Short coupled.

## Incorrect

**LONG COUPLED** but with correct length of back (in proportion to its height).

Rib Cage lacks depth at the last ribs so length of the loin is increased.

**Long in loin.**

## Incorrect

**LONG COUPLED**

Rib Cage deep and long which is correct but length of back too long, therefore the length of loin is increased. A weaker structure.

**Too long in loin.**

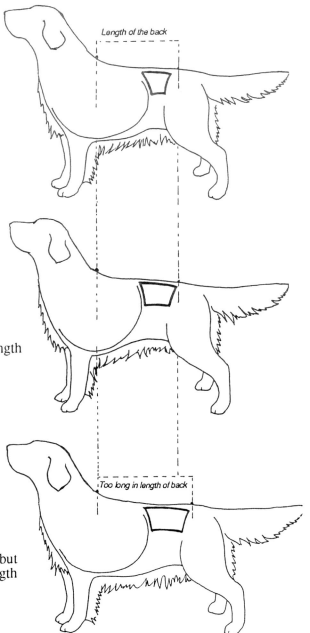

The Breed Standard
# The Body

* ***Level Topline***

# The Tail

* ***Set on and carried level with back***
* ***Reaching the hocks***
* ***Without curl at tip***

# Topline, Tailset & Tail Carriage

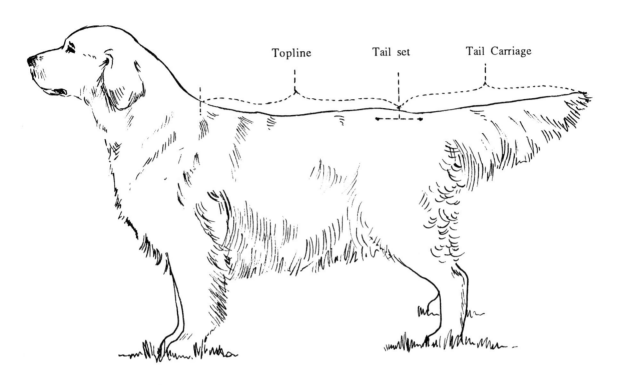

## Topline, Tail Set and Tail Carriage are interelated

They can, however, be assessed separately. It is possible to have a correct level topline, but with a tail set too high or too low, just as it is possible to have a correct topline and tail set, but with a tail carried incorrectly!

# The Topline

The topline is the back of the dog, from the withers to the croup, when viewed in profile.

The Breed standard requires THE TOPLINE TO BE LEVEL.

Although it should appear to be absolutely level visually, when the dog is handled one will discern a fractional rise over the pelvic area. Refer to the canine skeleton and you can see the reason for this.

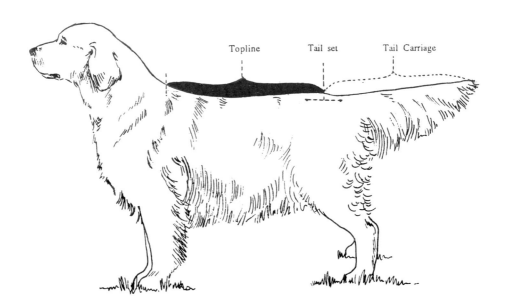

# The Topline

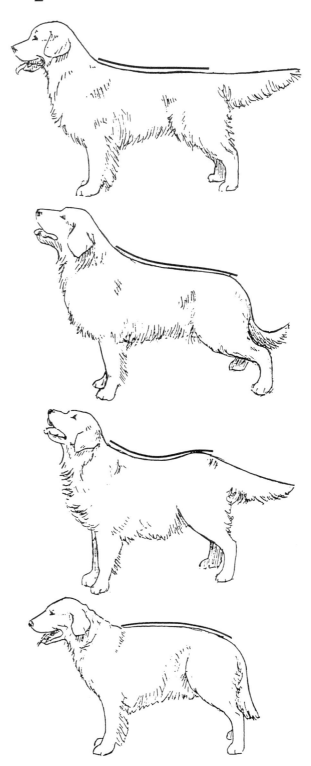

## Correct

**LEVEL TOPLINE**

Tail well-set on.
Tail carriage level.

## Incorrect

**SLOPING TOPLINE**

A downward slope from the withers to the croup.

## Incorrect

**DIPPING TOPLINE**

The backbone has a hollow between the withers and the pelvis showing a weak spine and poor muscular tone.

## Incorrect

**A ROACH BACK**

The back is upwardly arched.

# Tail Carriage

On the move the tail should be carried level with the back. It acts as a 'rudder' and balancing device as well as reflecting a dog's emotions! It should not be carried above the level of the back (Gay in tail) and certainly should not be curled over the back. Neither should it be carried low.

Sometimes a high tail carriage reflects a dog's 'mood', particularly in a young male. Likewise a low carriage or a tail curled under the body reflects a timid or apprehensive dog. Both are incorrect and must be assessed accordingly.

The length of the tail (bone and muscle, not feathering) to reach the hocks, and be without a curl at the tip.

The tail should be quite heavily muscled, particularly at the base, and be densely coated with long feathering.

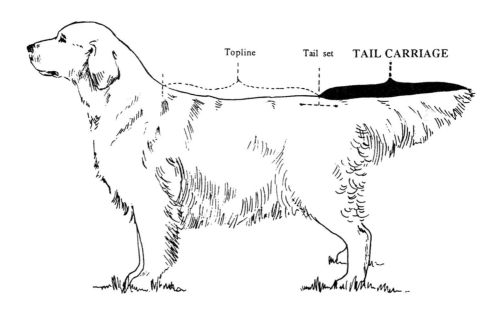

# Tail Carriage

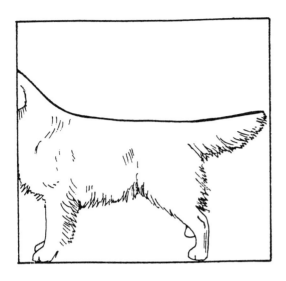

**Correct**

When on the move, the tail is carried level with the back.

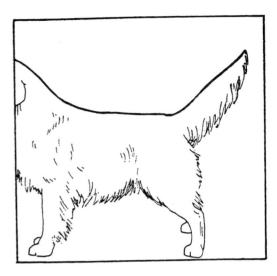

**Incorrect**

It should not be held above the level of the back.

**Incorrect**

It should not be curled over the back like an Afghan.

**Incorrect**

It should not be held curled under the body like a Whippet.

# *Tailset*

The tailset refers to the position that the Saccral bones of the tail have in relation to the vertebrae of the spine. The base of the tail at this point is also referred to as the Croup. (See page 60 - 61)

The *Tail set* refers to the point where the tail joins the body. It does not refer to the position that the tail is carried in, (see previous page) either in repose or when the dog is on the move.

Ideally, the tail is set on level with the back.

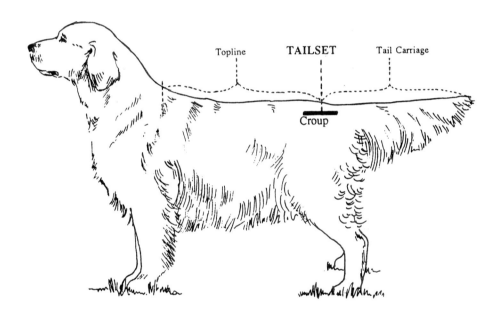

# Tail Set

## Correct

**LEVEL**

Tail well-set on and carried level with the back

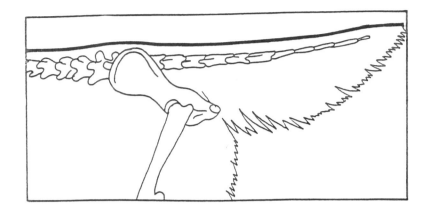

## Incorrect

**TOO HIGH**

Croup too level, making the tail set too high up on the back.

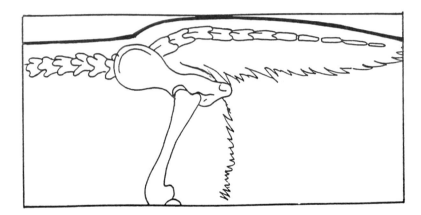

## Incorrect

**TOO LOW**

Croup too slanting. Tail set on too low.

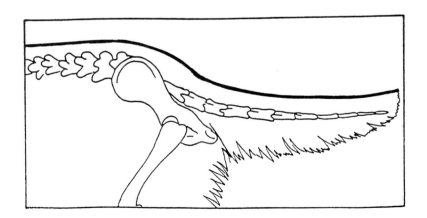

The Breed Standard
# Hindquarters

* Loin and legs strong and muscular

* Good second thighs

* Well bent stifles

* Hocks well let down

* Hocks straight when viewed from rear, neither turning in nor out

* Cow hocks highly undesirable

# Hindquarters

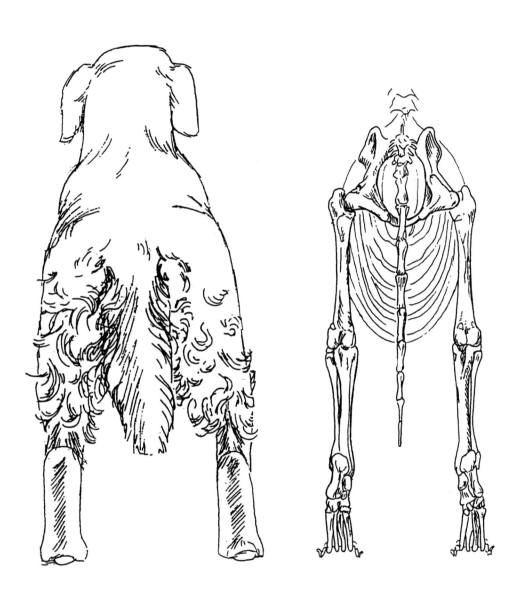

The Breed Standard
# Hindquarters

* *Hocks well let down*

* *Hocks straight when viewed from rear, neither turning in nor out*

* *Cow hocks highly undesirable*

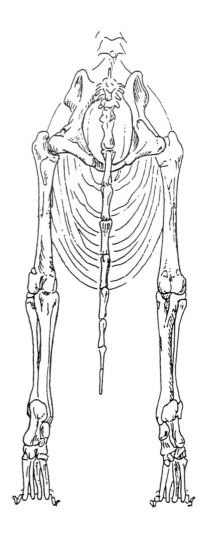

### Correct

**STRAIGHT PILLAR OF BONE** from hip to pad.

The feet are also straight. This is **correct**.

# Hindquarters

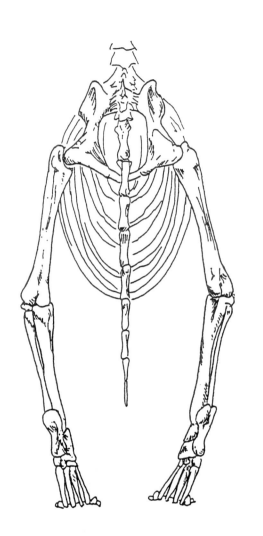 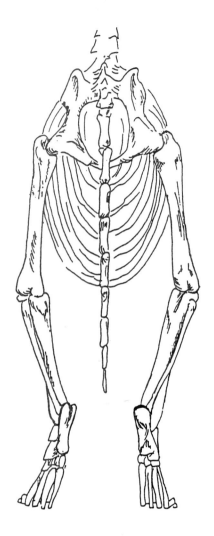

## Incorrect

**BOW LEGGED**
Straight line from hip to pad broken.

Hocks turning out.
Toes turning in.

## Incorrect

**COW HOCKED**
Straight line from hip to pad broken.

Hocks turning in.
Toes turning out.

# Angulation of the Hindquarters
## The Pelvis

The Pelvic structure forms a protective cavity which contains the reproductive organs and the bladder. It consists of the ileum, pubis and ischium. The pelvis is attached to the spine at the sacrum.

It is to the pelvis that the bones of the rear leg are attached - at the hip joint.

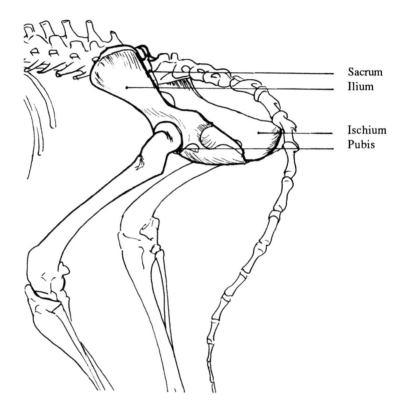

### Angle or tilt of the Pelvis

The angle or tilt of the pelvis, which is aboyt 30°from the horizontal affects not only the tail set - high, level or low - but also the angle of attachment of the hind limbs in the hip socket and therefore the angle that the legs are placed under the body.

### Slope of the Croup

The slope of croup is much less than the slope of the pelvis. It is the area between the top of the pelvis and the base of the tail. In profile the slope will appear very slight.

# The Pelvis

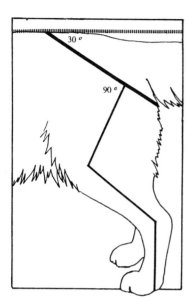

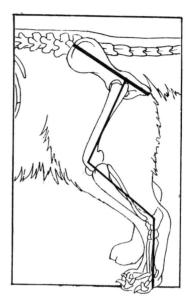

### Correct
The angle of the pelvis is set at approx. 30° from the horizontal. In a natural stance the femur joins the pelvis at about a 90° angle.

### Correct
A correctly angled croup, with a level tail set, well bent stifles and hocks vertical to the ground.

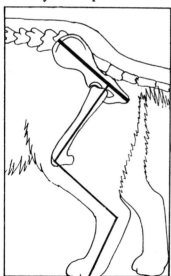

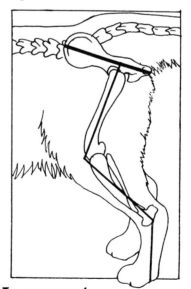

### Incorrect
The pelvis is too steeply angled. This pushes the legs well under the body and makes the dog appear to be crouching. The tail is set is too low as a result.

### Incorrect
The pelvis is too shallowly angled. This raises the bottom up. The tail is set on too high as a result.

The Breed Standard
# *Hindquarters*

* *Loin and legs strong and muscular*

* *Good second thighs*

* *Well bent stifle*

# Stifle Angulation

*The angulation of the rear quarters should echo and balance the angulation of the fore quarters.*

The stifles should be 'well bent' with an angle of approximately 90° at the knee joint. Too much of an angle - over angulation - will weaken the structure.

**The hindquarters provide the power and drive. They should be well muscled.** Strong muscles feel hard and firm to the touch. They should not feel soft, spongy or flabby.

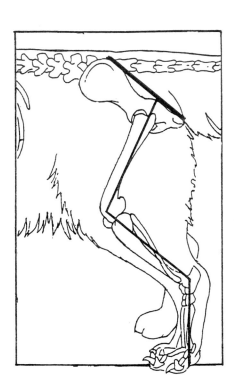 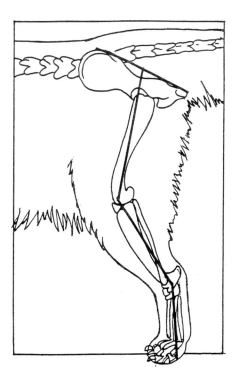

## Correct

**WELL ANGULATED STIFLE**

With well developed and muscular thighs. This structure allows for optimum power and motive force from the rear quarters.

## Incorrect

**STRAIGHT IN STIFLE**

The lack of angulation will limit the backward extension of the leg and therefore restrict 'drive' from the rear.

The Breed Standard
# *Hindquarters*

*   *Hocks well let down*

*   *Hocks straight when viewed from rear, neither turning in nor out*

*   *Cow hocks highly undesirable*

# *Hocks* *seen from the side*

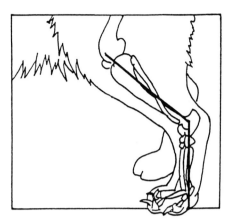

### *Correct*
Dog standing with hocks vertical to the ground.
Straight when viewed from side and/or rear.
Good angulation into stifle.
It is desirable to have hocks 'well let down' or 'short in hock' as they give strength to the lever that is formed by the hock bone and the metatarsals.

The hock bone itself cannot be short, so the phrase is rather erroneous. The metatarsals must not be overlong

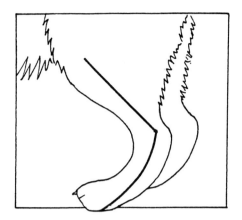

### *Incorrect*
Sickle Hocks.

The hock curves under the body causing the back part of the foot to be walked on and not the front part of the pads. This is a sign of weakness.

An over angulated hock, as in a sickle hock, places the foot too far under the body, but the hock itself may not be bowed

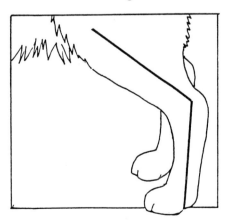

### *Incorrect*
Too long in hock.
Hocks and metatarsal bones overlong, weakening the structure.

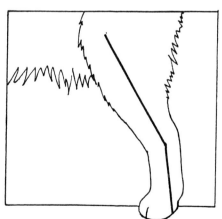

### *Incorrect*
Straight in hock.
A lack of angulation at the hock joint impedes leverage.

The Breed Standard
# *The Feet*

\* *Round and cat-like*

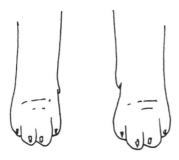 

**Correct**

Round and Cat like.

**Incorrect**

Splay feet

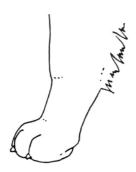 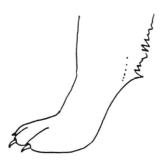

**Correct**

Cat foot.
Compact with arched toes
and well developed pads.
Nails short.

**Incorrect**

Hare foot.
Toes long and flat.
Nails too long.

# Pasterns

## *The pasterns act as shock absorbers*

The pastern consists of five long metacarpel bones of which only four are used. The fifth ends in a dew claw, which is equivalent to a man's thumb. The front bones of the pastern bear a dog's weight but do not provide for any leverage.

Together with thick, well developed pads on the feet they cushion against the impact of landing, helping to keep the head (and brain) steady.

It is generally accepted that for the greatest efficiency in absorbing shock, the pastern should be short and strong and sloping slightly from the vertical.

### PASTERN JOINTS

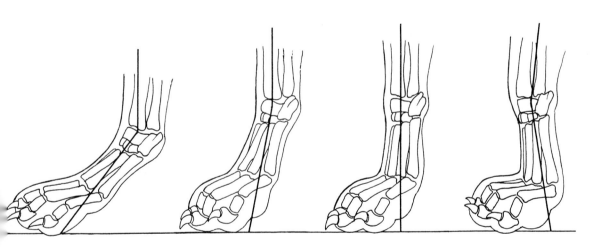

*Incorrect*

Pastern broken-down with displaced bones and poor muscle tone. A weak pastern.

*Correct*

Pastern with the correct slope, and with no suggestion of weakness. Effective for shock absorbancy.

*Incorrect*

Straight pastern. This pastern will not absorb shock as well as a sloping one.

*Incorrect*

Knuckled-over. A weak pastern.

If the pastern is too straight the legs will knuckle over at the group of bones at the pastern joint (Carpus) and the whole leg will the start to quiver, owing to the extra strain put on the muscles.

The Breed Standard
# *Size*

* **Height at withers:**
  **Dogs :**        **56 - 61cms (22 - 24 inches)**
  **Bitches :**   **51 - 56 cms (20 - 22 inches)**

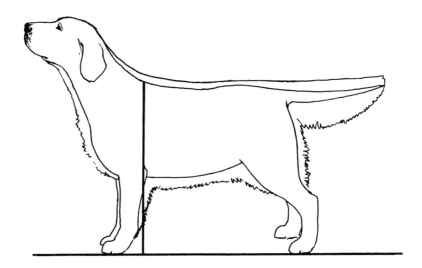

*Height is measured from the top of the withers (the scapula bone under the hair) to the ground.*

The limits of height were set to keep the Golden Retriever of a size to most efficiently perform his required work. He is large and powerful enough to negotiate all sorts of obstacles and terrain - including water. He is strong enough to handle, lift and carry all species of game, both fur and feathered. He is not cumbersome, yet he is built for endurance and moderate speed. He remains small enough to be agile and of a convenient size to have in a hide, a boat or a car.

# Weight & Condition
## *The Standard used to, but no longer refers to an optimum weight*

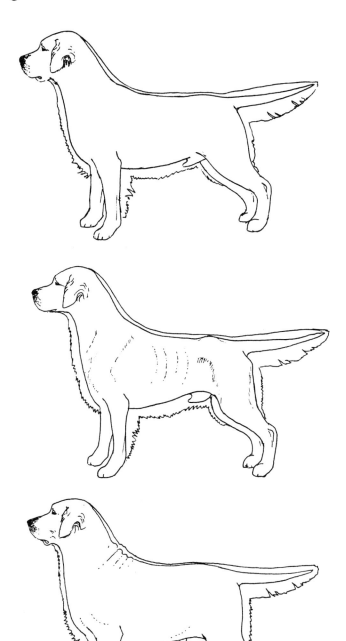

## Correct

**HARD WORKING CONDITION**

Firm, well developed muscles, lean rather than plump. A slight covering of fat, properly distributed, contributes to the quality of skin and coat. It also provides insulation against cold and is a useful energy resource during periods of stress.

A retriever should never be flabby and lean is far preferable to fat.

## Incorrect

**UNDERWEIGHT**

Angular and gaunt with bones prominent, particularly over the loin and rib cage. The underweight dog has less reserve capacity for stress than a dog in optimum condition.

## Incorrect

**TOO FAT**

Excess fat over the loin and shoulders obscures the proper outline. Excess weight may cause structural weaknesses like broken down pasterns or push the elbows out. The dog will not be able to work effectively and will tire easily.

The Breed Standard
# *Faults*

* *Any departure from the foregoing points should be considered a fault and the seriousness with which the fault should be regarded should be in exact proportion to its degree*

*Note*

* *Male animals should have two apparently normal testicals fully descended into the scrotum*

# Faults

## The perfect dog has yet to be born!

If the construction of the dog differs from the ideal as stated in the Standard, then that dog has a fault. The judge is looking to see how closely the dog fits the Standard; he is not making a list of how many faults each dog possesses. To fault-judge is quite wrong.

The U.K. Standard states that...

> *"......the seriousness with which the fault should be regarded should be in exact proportion to its degree"*

It does not state if some faults are more serious than others, although some obviously are. The American Standard is more helpful as it specifies...

> *"Any departure from the described ideal shall be considered faulty to the degree to which it interferes with the breed's purpose or is contary to breed character."*

The 'purpose' of the breed as a working gundog is to retrieve dead and wounded game in the field, so any fault which hinders or interferes with this functional aspect must be regarded very seriously indeed. A constructional fault like cow-hocks, where the rear assembly is weak and lacks power and drive, should be more heavily penalised, than for example, a lighter than ideal eye or a temporary lack of coat and feathering,.

Variations from the ideal are endless. In judging one has to assess the relative importance of each fault and to place the dogs in some order of merit.

The job of judging is often not an easy one.

Any fault in temperament, where a dog or bitch shows unprovoked hostility or aggression or undue timidity, is contary to breed character and should be heavily penalised.

The Breed Standard
# The Coat

* *Flat or wavy with good feathering*

* *Dense water-resistent undercoat*

## The Coat

*The Golden Retriever has a distinctive double coat providing protection against heavy cover and keeping him both warm and dry. It may be either straight or wavy.*

**Top Coat.** Firm resilient hair lying close to the body to form a weatherproof jacket. It should not be as silky as a setter's or stiff and hard to the touch but should have good body and be firm enough to resist most tangles and burrs. It should lie parallel to the body to enable water to run off easily.

**Undercoat.** A thick soft woolly undercoat made up of hairs of 1-1 1/2 inches long. The density of the undercoat should insulate and prevent water penetrating to the skin.

**Feathering.** The hair on the back of forelegs and on the underpart of the body will be longer than body coat forming a softer fringe. Featherings on tail, back of thighs and ruff around neck and chest will have a thick undercoat. Coat on head, ears and fronts of legs should be smooth and short, yet still dense and thick with an undercoat.

**Out of coat.** Periodically and especially in warmer weather a Golden will lose his undercoat and part of his topcoat. Bitches after having puppies will lose most of it! A coat 'on the blow' (beginning to fall out) will become dull and lack lustre. It varies, but generally it takes around two months for the new coat to grow back in. An 'out of coat' dog is at a temporary disadvantage in the showring.

**A curly coat** - rarely seen nowadays, except in some field trial strains - is quite incorrect. Do not confuse this with a very wavy coat with a 'flick' of a curl in it, particularly after bathing. A curly coat has tight curls, sometimes ringlets, all over the back and feathering and is incapable of lying flat. A throw-back to the coat of the Tweed Water Spanial possibly.

**Photograph on opposite page.**
**An Example of dogs with a straight coat and a wavy coat. Both equally acceptable.**

The Breed Standard
# *Colour*

* ***Any shade of gold or cream***

* ***Neither red nor mahogany***

* ***A few white hairs on chest permissible***

## Colour

The colour is darkest on ears, back and body with lighter parts on the feathering of underparts, 'knickers' and tail plume. Variations in shadings of the coat are quite acceptable.

White markings have definite borders and are not to be confused with lighter shadings of the coat. These are often found as a spot on the forehead or white on the toes and are undesirable and to be faulted. Black spots on the coat ranging in size from a few hairs to an obvious splotch are rare, but are also faulty.

A young puppy will darker to the colour of its ears as it matures and changes coat.
In older dogs, some whiten and become grey around the muzzle and eyes, and along the back, especially those which have darker coats. This a natural process and not a sign of decrepitude, and a dog should not be penalized for this.

Pigmentation of the skin is not related to hair pigmentation. The skin of the body can range from pinky white to nearly black. Good pigmentation will be evident in black eye-rims, nose and edges of the lips, feet pads and nails. Less good pigmentation will result in some noses that fade in the winter to a speckled brown. A distinctly pink nose or lack of pigmentation around eye rims to be faulted as this spoils the expression.

**Photograph on opposite page, from left to right.**

**Incorrect.**  The pure white coat of the Samoyed.
**Correct.**  The range of colour from cream to dark gold of the four centre Golden Retrievers.
**Incorrect.**  The red / mahogoney colour of the Irish Setter.

The Breed Standard
# Gait - Movement

* **Powerful with good drive**

* **Straight and true in front and rear**

* **Stride long and free with no sign of hackney action in front**

# Movement
## Line of convergence

When a dog moves from standing and increases speed, his legs, when seen from front or rear, must incline towards the mid-line to maintain balance and grace and for maximum efficiency in movement. If on the move, the limbs remained parallel to the mid-line, the gait would be clumsy, and produce a slight roll of the shoulders.

The faster a dog moves, the more his legs will incline inwards until the speed is reached where he will single track in order to maintain balance.

The line of bones from the shoulder to the foot and from the hip to the foot must be in a straight line, but the line is not a vertical line (except when standing).

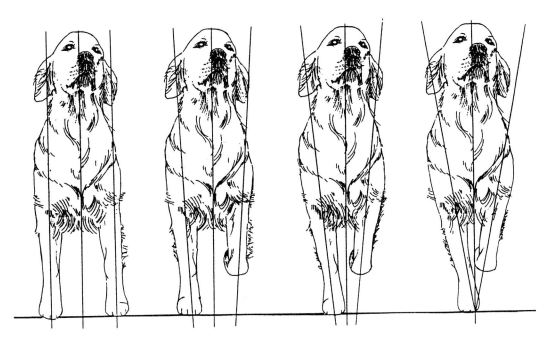

**Standing**     **Slow Trot**     **Trot**     **At Speed**

Line from shoulder to pad vertical.

Line from shoulder to pad is straight, but slightly inclined to the central line.

*In the ring a dog is moved between a slow trot and a trot.*

Line from shoulder to pad is straight, but inclining more to the central line.

Legs are still in a straight line but inclining even more to the centre. The foot will not touch the weight bearing leg as it flexes and passes above it.

# Movement

## Single Tracking

The difference between 'single tracking' and 'moving close' needs to be clearly understood. It is the difference between a sound dog and an unsound one.

When a dog is moving at speed his legs will angle in towards the central line and he will place each pad in a straight line one with the other. This is single tracking.

The forward moving leg will not touch or clip the weight-bearing leg as it passes it, because it is flexed and passes above it. If the forward moving leg does interfere with the weight bearing leg, than there is a constructional fault in the dog and the alignment of bones and joints will not be in a straight line. It may also be due to a fault in timing.

## Moving Close

'Moving close' may still mean that the feet fall in a single line or track, but the movement is an unsound one. When seen from the front or rear, the column of bones from shoulder to pad or from hip to pad, are not in a straight line but are broken in one or two places. This reduces efficiency and economy of effort and uses more energy.

From the rear it may be the hocks which break the straight line. This is seen in the cow hocked dog. This fault is a great weakness and specifically mentioned in the Breed Standard as undesirable.

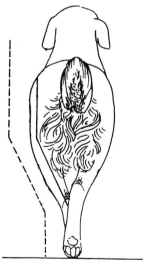

*Incorrect*

**MOVING CLOSE**

The straight line is broken in two places.

# Rear Movement

## The Hind limbs provide the majority of the motive power

The shock absorbing aspects of the hind limb are particularly important because, unlike the forelimb, the hind leg is directly attached to the spine through the pelvis and sacrum, and power needs to be applied smoothly to ensure the motive power, provided by the limb, is transmitted efficiently to the spine and thus moves the body forward without jerking the head.

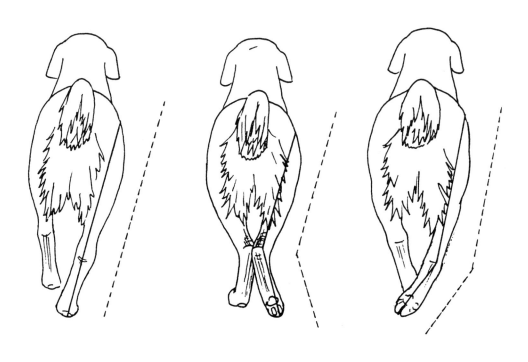

**Correct**

**Incorrect**

**Incorrect**

**FAST TROT**

**COW HOCKED**

**HOCKS SLOPE INWARDS**

Straight line from hip to pad. Lines converging to centre is correct.

Straight line from hip to pad broken at the hock.

Straight line from hip to pad broken at the hock.

# Front Movement

## The foreleg assembly is designed to carry weight and to act as a shock absorber

The foreleg assembly supports over half the body weight and absorbs the impact of landing (preventing the brain from shock and ensuring that the head is moved forward in a steady and efficient manner).

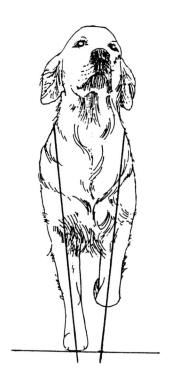

**Correct**

**TROT**

Straight line from shoulder
to foot pad.

# Front Movement

*It is worth remembering that the forelimb is connected to the body simply by muscle*

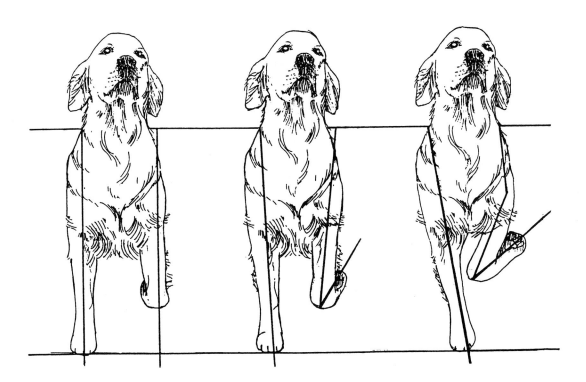

**Incorrect**

**PARALLEL**

Tight at the shoulders. Ungainly rolling action.

**Incorrect**

**WINGING/PADDLING**

Bone alignment is broken at the pasterns.

**Incorrect**

**WEAVING**

Straight line is broken at the elbows and pasterns.

# *Movement* *as seen from the side*

*The sequence of a stride in slow motion in 5 parts*

### Part 1
He is reaching forward and supported on the left front leg and its diagonal hind leg as he drives off the right hind foot.

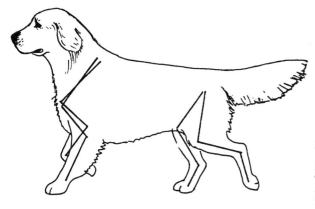

### Part 2
The body is carried forward over the supporting legs by the motion.
The right front leg and its diagonal hind leg is lifted up and brought forward.

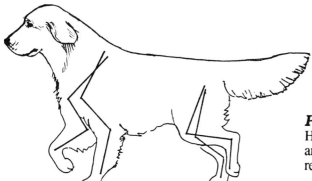

### Part 3
His body has continued to move forward and here his legs are collected under him ready to begin a new thrust.

# *Movement* as seen from the side

## Continued

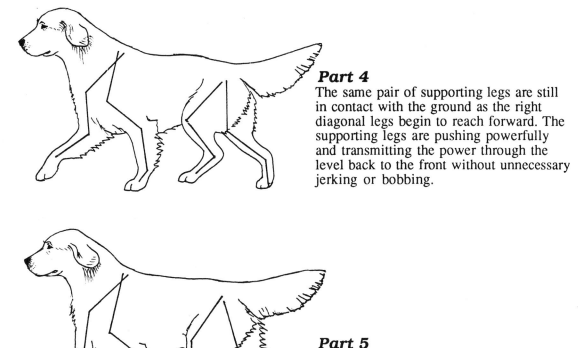

### Part 4
The same pair of supporting legs are still in contact with the ground as the right diagonal legs begin to reach forward. The supporting legs are pushing powerfully and transmitting the power through the level back to the front without unnecessary jerking or bobbing.

### Part 5
Legs now fully extended. The right diagonal pair of legs is just about to make contact with the ground. The next phase of the stride would be identical but using the opposite pair of legs.

The great length of stride is made possible by the properly angulated limbs and by the 'opening-up' of the shoulder and stifle assemblies.

Notice how the timing of the forefeet is a fraction ahead of the hindfeet. You will notice in Part 5 particularly, that the forefoot has left the ground in time for the hindfoot on the same side to land on the same track without striking it.

Without this timing the dog would have three alternatives in order to avoid hitting his forefeet:
Move the hindfeet to the side - crabbing or side tracking, move wide behind or to shorten the stride considerably.

# Movement

*There are three anatomical systems involved with movement.*

>**Bones and Joints**
>**Muscles**
>**The Nervous System**

## The Bones and Joints

*The bones make up the skeleton but it is the interconnection between the bones - The Joints - that have the bigger part to play in movement.*

Joints basically articulate in two ways: A ball and socket joint or a hinge joint.

**The shoulder and hip joints are both ball and socket joints.** They allow the plane of movement to be backwards and forwards, side to side as well as to rotate.

**The elbow and wrist in the forelimb and the stifle and hock in the rear limb are hinge joints** allowing a backwards and forwards movement only. In the lower limb there is a capability to modify the movement by an ability to twist the foot slightly by a rotation in the forearm of the radius and ulna, and in the rear limb the tibia and fibula.

The limits of shoulder articulation determine the length of stride. The ability of the forelimb to move upwards and outwards is limited and controlled by the muscles of the shoulder, for these effectively bind and link the limb to the body.

The hip joint is the principal point of rotation responsible for moving the dog forward.

# Movement - The Joints

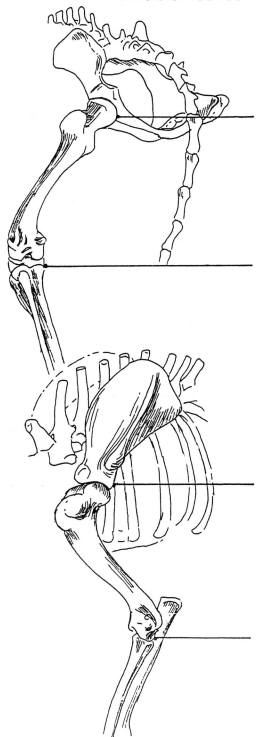

### The Hip Joint

**A Ball and Socket Joint**

Allows limb to swing back and forth, side to side (as in cocking a leg) and to rotate.

### The Stifle Joint

**A Hinge Joint**

Similar to that of the elbow. Allows backward and forward action but not from side to side.

**The Hock Joint is also a Hinge Joint**

### The Shoulder Joint

**A shallow Ball and Socket Joint**

Allows similar movement to that of the hip.

### The Elbow Joint

**A Hinge Joint**

Allows the limb to close the angle forwards, but not to extend backwards or go from side to side.

**The Wrist Joint is also a Hinge Joint**

# Movement - The Muscles

## The Muscles provide the power to move the skeleton

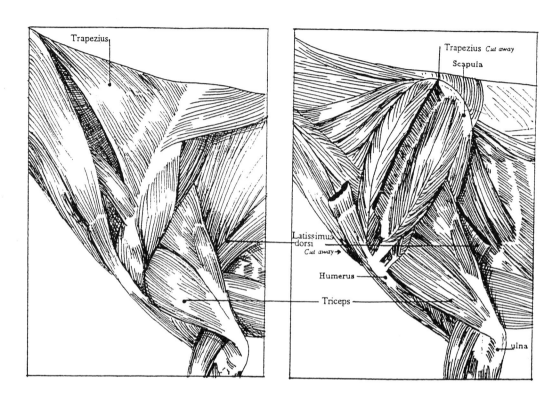

**1. Muscles of the Shoulder**
The top layer of muscles - the cutaneous - have been cut away to reveal this, the next layer in. There are layers beneath this too. See Diagram 2.

**2. Muscles of the Shoulder**
In this diagram some major muscles have been cut away to reveal still deeper muscles underneath.

***These diagrams serve to illustrate the complexity of the muscular structure.***

Muscles are attached to the bones by ligaments, and expand and contract - rather like elastic. Because most of the bones need to move in more than one direction there are muscles to pull and push up and down, and to swing or twist them from side to side. That is why there are so many overcrossing layers.

As far as the Breed Standard is concerned understanding which muscle goes under or over which other muscle in their many layers, is not an issue.

*But it is vitally important to realise their dramatic affect on movement. Under - developed muscles, poor or slack muscular tone, or even too much muscle (i.e. over-loaded shoulders) will result in poor movement.*

# Movement

## Muscles

*These contract to move the bones which in turn pivot around the joints.*

*Each and every muscle operates by contracting and expanding.*

To move a limb, the flexor muscle will contract to close the angle of the joint, while the extensor will allow the limb to be expanded. These two muscles work against each other around the joint. If they both contract at the same time the joint will be fixed, which is how a dog stands up. All the joints in the limb being fixed by equal and opposite muscle tone in the opposing muscles. Thus standing requires energy. In standing the joints are fixed and angulated in a position that the dog finds most comfortable.

## The Nervous System

*Muscles do not operate independently, they are co-ordinated and powered by the nervous system which synchronise their contractions.*

It is the impulses from sensitive receptors in muscles, joints and tendons that inform the brain how the limb is positioned and the brain then dictates which muscles need to contract to move the limb.

The whole process is automated and controlled by the part of the brain called the Cerebellum. However, a lot of limb responses are controlled by the spinal cord with the brain modifying them at will.

# The Development of the Golden Retriever Breed Standard

### English and American

# The Golden Retriever Breed Standard

## The early days...

### 1908

When Golden Retrievers were first exhibited in 1908 they were not classified by the Kennel Club as a distinct breed, but only as a variety of Retriever. They were shown in mixed classes for Flat-coated (or Wavy-coated) Retrievers "of any colour".

### 1911

In 1906, Mrs Charlesworth (Noranby) obtained her first Golden, a bitch called Normanby Beauty. She proved to be a highly intelligent and tireless worker. In 1909 Mrs Charlesworth decided to try showing her too and joined Lord Hardcourt, who was then winning with Culham Copper, Culham Brass and Culham Tip as the only other exhibitor of the "yellow" dogs, at Crufts 1909. Although th, and ten in 1910.
However, in 1911, Mrs Charleswoth's enthusiasm overcame all difficulties and, with a few other enthusiasts, she founded the Golden Retriever Club, which drew up a Standard of points. In the same year the Kennel Club officially gave the breed classification as a separate variety of Retrievers under the title of "Golden or Yellow Retrievers"

When the Golden Retriever Club first drew up the Standard in 1911 (see next page), a scale of points was included as a rough guide to the relative importance of its features. This was not intended to be used as a method of scoring each dog when judging. Although obviously very important, you will note that no points at all were allocated to general appearance or movement. At that time, it was taken for granted that judges had a working knowledge of the dogs' basic structure and functions, and that it must also move properly.

Then, the emphasis was on establishing a breed type of some consistency and the qualities relating to that goal were given priority. Great importance was placed on the head, the body, coat and colour as the features that were unique to the Golden and which set it apart from the other retriever breeds.

# The First British Breed Standard - 1911

|  |  | Maximum Points |
|---|---|---|
| *General Appearance* | Should be of a symmetrical, active, powerful dog, a good level mover, sound and well put together, with a kindly expression, not clumsy nor long in the leg. | |
| *Head.* | Broad skull, well set on a clean and muscular neck, muzzle powerful and wide, not weak-jawed, good stop.<br>*Eyes.*<br>Dark, and set well apart, very kindly expression, with dark rims.<br>*Teeth.*<br>Even, neither under nor overshot............................................ | 20 |
| *Ears* | Well proportioned, of moderate size and well set on................. | 5 |
| *Nose* | Should be black, but a light-coloured one should not debar a dog from honours who is good in all other respects........................ | 5 |
| *Colour* | Rich golden, must not be as dark as the Irish Setter, nor cream coloured. The presence of a few white hairs on chest or toes permissible. (White collar or blaze to be penalised)................. | 20 |
| *Coat.* | Should be flat or wavy with good feathering, and dense, water resisting undercoat............................................................. | 5 |
| *Feet* | Round and cat-like, not open or splay.................................... | 10 |
| *Fore-legs* | Straight with good bone...................................................... | 10 |
| *Hind-legs* | Strong and muscular, stifles well bent. Hocks well let down, not cow-hocked................................................................ | 10 |
| *Tail* | Should not be carried too gay or curled at the tip..................... | 5 |
| *Body* | Well-balanced, short coupled and deep through the heart. Loins should be strong, ribs deep and well sprung. Shoulders should be well laid back and long in the blade........................ | 25 |
| | Total | 115 |

Note: The average weight for dogs in good hard condition should be:
Dogs 65 - 70 lbs.   Bitches 56 - 60 lbs.
Height at shoulder:   Dogs 22 - 24 in.   Bitches 20 - 22 in.

# The Standard in 1936

During the 1920's into the early 1930's, the darker dogs were much more popular than the light gold ones. The lighter dogs gradually gained acceptance and were acknowledged by the admission of 'cream' in the Standard in about 1936.
The wording was changed to:

*Colour*   *Any shade of gold or cream, but neither red nor mahogany. The presence of a few white hairs on chest permissible. White collar, feet, toes or blaze to be penalised.*

# In the 1940s

The Kennel Club's official Standard for the breed issued in the 1940s omitted the scale of points and the words immediately following 'nose should be black'. It changed the misleading "Teeth should be even" to...

*Mouth*   *Teeth should be sound and strong. Neither undershot nor overshot, the lower teeth just behind but touching the upper teeth.*

The Breed Standard remained essentially the same for 30 or more years, until in the 1990's, when the Kennel Club reviewed all their Standards, they made small changes to the format. Also, although the ideal height remains, the ideal weight of a dog and a bitch has been omitted.

# The American Breed Standard

The original English Breed Standard of 1911 was also used in the United States until the 1950's when it was revised because it was felt that it was lacking in many respects. There was a real concern about the number of very tall dogs being shown and winning extensively. The oversize dog was recognised by those who worked their Goldens as being absolutely contrary to working efficiency and breed type, yet they were eye-catching and stylish in the show ring, and the trend was seen as a real threat to the breed's best interests.

A completely new Standard was adopted in late 1954. For the first time the judge was to disqualify from competition any Golden Retriever who was over or under size, had over or undershot jaws, or had the eye problems of trichiasis or entropion. Monorchids and cryptorchids were to be disqualified as well.

In 1979 a committee was appointed by the GRCA to expand and clarify the wording used to describe the ideal Golden Retriever as in the 1954 Standard. By 1981 the revision was completed and approved by the American Kennel Club.

In 1990 the AKC felt a need to get all breed Standards - over 120 of them - into a uniform format as they varied wildly in presentation. A 'cut and paste' job took place to the Golden Retriever one with as little wording changed as possible. This is the Standard currently in effect in the U.S.

# The American Breed Standard for the Golden Retriever
*Reproduced by kind permission of the American Kennel Club*

## General Appearance

A Symmetrical, powerful active dog, sound and well put together, not clumsy nor long in the leg, displaying a kindly expression and possessing a personality that is eager, alert and self-confident. Primarily a hunting dog, he should be shown in hard working condition. Overall appearance, balance, gait and purpose to be given more emphasis than any of its component parts.

## Head

Broad in skull, slightly arched laterally and longitudinally without prominence of frontal bones or occipital bones. Stop well defined but not abrupt. Foreface deep and wide, nearly as long as skull. Muzzle straight in profile, blending smoothly and strongly into skull; when viewed in profile or from above, slightly deeper and wider at stop than at tip. No heaviness in flews. Removal of whiskers is permitted but not preferred.

## Eyes

Friendly and intelligent in expression, medium size with dark, close-fitting rim, set well apart and reasonably deep in sockets. Color preferably dark brown, medium brown acceptable. Slant eyes and narrow, triangular eyes detract from correct expression and are to be faulted. No white or haw visible when looking straight ahead. Dogs showing function abnormality of eyelids or eyelashes (such as, but not limited to, trichiasis, entropion, ectropion or distichiasis) are to be excused from the ring.

## Nose

Black or brownish in color, though fading to a lighter shade in cold weather not serious. Pink nose or one seriously lacking in pigmentation to be faulted.

## Ears

Rather short with front edge attached well behind and just above the eye and falling close to cheek. When pulled forward, tip of ear should just cover the eye. Low, hound-like ear set to be faulted.

## Neck

Medium long, merging gradually into well laid shoulders, giving a sturdy muscular appearance. Untrimmed natural ruff. No throatiness.

# Breed Standard  Kennel Club of America

## Body

Well balanced, short coupled, deep through chest. Chest between forelegs at least as wide as a man's closed hand, including thumb, with well-developed forechest. Brisket extends to elbows. Ribs long and well sprung but not barrel-shaped, extending well towards hindquarters. Loin short, muscular, wide and deep with very little tuck-up. Back line strong and level from withers to slightly sloping croup whether standing or moving. Slab-sidedness, narrow chest, lack of depth of brisket, sloping back line, roach or sway back, excessive tuck-up, flat or steep croup to be faulted.

## Forequarters

Muscular, well co-ordinated with hindquarters, and capable of free movement. Shoulder blades long and well laid back with upper tips fairly close together at withers. Upper arms appear about the same length as the blades, setting the elbows back beneath the upper tip of the blades, close to the ribs without looseness. Legs viewed from the front, straight with good bone but not to the point of coarseness. Pasterns short and strong, sloping slightly with no suggestion of weakness.

## Hindquarters

Broad and strong muscled. Profile of croup slopes slightly; the pelvic bone slopes at a slightly greater angle (approximately 30° from the horizontal). In a natural stance, the femur joins the pelvis at approximately a 90° angle; stifles well bent; hocks well let down with short, strong neat pasterns, Legs straight when viewed from rear. Cow hocks, spread hocks and sickle hocks to be faulted.

## Feet

Medium size, round and compact and well knuckled, with thick pads. Excess hair may be trimmed to show size and contour. Dewclaws on forelegs may be removed but are normally left on. Splay or hare feet to be faulted.

## Tail

Well set on, thick and muscular at the base, following the natural line of the croup. Tail bones extend to, but not below, the point of the hock carried with a merry action, level with or some moderate upward curve, never curled over back or between legs.

## Coat

Dense and water repellant with good undercoat. Outer coat firm and resilient, neither coarse nor silky, lying close to the body; may be straight or wavy. Moderate feathering on back of forelegs and on under-body; heavier feathering on front of neck, back of thighs and underside of tail. Coat on head, paws and front of legs is short and even. Excessive length, open coats and limp, soft coats are very undesirable. Feet may be trimmed and stray hair neatened, but the natural appearance of coat or outline should not be altered by cutting or clipping.

# Breed Standard Kennel Club of America

## Color

Rich, lustrous golden of various shades. Feathering may be lighter than rest of coat. With the exception of greying or whitening of face or body due to age, any white marking, other than a few white hairs on the chest, should be penalized according to its extent. Allowable light shadings not to be confused with white marking. Predominant body color which is extremely pale or extremely dark is undesirable. Some latitude should be given to the light puppy whose coloring shows promise of deepening with maturity. Any noticeable area of black or other off-color hair is a serious fault.

## Gait

When trotting, gait is free, smooth, powerful and well co-ordinated, showing good reach. Viewed from any position, legs turn neither in nor out, nor do feet cross or interfere with each other. As speed increases, feet tend to converge towards centre line of balance. It is recommended that dogs be shown on a loose lead to reflect true gait.

## Size

Males 23-24 inches in height at withers; females 21 1/2 - 22 1/2. Dogs up to one inch above or below standard size should be proportionately penalised. Deviation in height of more than one inch from the Standard shall disqualify. Length from breastbone to point of buttocks slightly greater than height at withers in ratio of 12:11. Weight of dogs 65-75 lbs; bitches 55-65 lbs.

## Temperament

Friendly, reliable and trustworthy. Quarrelsomeness or hostility towards other dogs or people in normal situations, or an unwarranted show of timidity or nervousness, is not in keeping with Golden Retriever character. Such actions should be penalized according to their significance.

## Faults

Any departure from the described ideal shall be considered faulty to the degree to which it interferes with the breed's purpose or is contrary to breed character.

## Disqualifications

1. Deviation in height of more than one inch from Standard either way.
2. Undershot or overshot bite.
3. Monorchids and cryptorchids to be disqualified (AKC rule applying to all breeds).

# *Terminology*

## *Glossary of terms used when Judging*

| | |
|---|---|
| **Angulation** | The angles formed at a joint by the meeting of the bones. |
| **Balance** | A consistent whole; symmetrical, typically proportioned as a whole or as regards its separate parts i.e. balance of head, balance of body. |
| **Bitchy** | A feminine looking male dog. |
| **Bite** | The relative position of the upper and lower teeth when the mouth is closed (level bite, scissor bite, undershot and overshot bite). |
| **Bodied up** | Matured, well developed. |
| **Bone** | The relative girth of the dog's leg bones. |
| **Bossy** | Loaded, heavy shoulders. Over development of the shoulder muscles. |
| **Breast bone** | Bone forming the floor of the chest. |
| **Brisket** | The forepart of the body below the chest between and slightly behind the elbows. |
| **Castrate** | To remove the testicles of the male dog. |
| **Cat foot** | Short, round, compact foot like that of a cat. |
| **Chippendale** | Refers to a front with forelegs out at the elbows, pasterns close and feet turned out. |
| **Chiselled** | Clean cut, showing bone structure of foreface. |
| **Close coupled** | Short in coupling and loin. |
| **Coarse** | Lacking refinement. Overdone in head and/or bone. |
| **Cobby** | Very short bodied, too compact. |
| **Conformation** | The form and structure, and the arrangements of the parts. |
| **Cowlick** | Incorrect lay of fur on the face often between the eyes. |
| **Cow hocked** | When the hocks turn inwards towards each other. |
| **Crabbing** | Dog moves with body at an angle to the line of travel. |

# Terminology

## Glossary of Terms used when Judging

| | |
|---|---|
| **Crossing over** | Unsound gaiting action which starts with twisting elbows and ends with crisscrossing and toeing out. Also called weaving. |
| **Cryptorchid** | An adult male whose testicles are abnormally retained in the abdominal cavity. |
| **Daylight** | The light showing underneath body. |
| **Dentition** | The number and arrangement of teeth. |
| **Dewclaw** | Fifth digit on the inside of the legs. |
| **Doggy** | A masculine looking bitch. |
| **Double coat** | An outer coat resistant to weather, together with an undercoat of softer hair for warmth and waterproofing. |
| **Down at Pasterns** | Weak or faulty metacarpus, set at a prounced angle from the vertical. |
| **Drive** | A powerful thrusting of the hindquarters, denoting sound locomotion. |
| **Dudley** | Liver, brown or putty coloured, used to describe poor nose pigment. |
| **Foreface** | The front part of the head, before the eyes. Muzzle. |
| **Furrow** | A slight indentation or median line from stop to occiput. |
| **Gay tail** | The tail carried high over the dog's back. Higher than approved in the standard. |
| **Hackney-action** | The high lifting of the front feet. |
| **Harefoot** | An elongated foot like that of a hare. |
| **Haw** | The third eyelid or membrane in the inside corner of the eye. |
| **Layback** | The angle of the shoulder blade when viewed from the side. |
| **Leather** | The flap of the ear. |
| **Leggy** | Too long in leg for correct balance. |
| **Loaded Shoulders** | When the shoulder blades are pushed out from the body. Over development of the muscles. |

# Terminology

## Glossary of terms used when Judging

| | |
|---|---|
| **Monorchid** | A dog with only one testicle in the scrotum. |
| **Moult** | Casting of the coat. |
| **Mouth** | The upper part and lower jaw bones containing the teeth. Also used to describe the bite i.e. 'a good mouth' or 'a bad mouth'. Sometimes used in retrieving parlance to describe the ability of a dog when carrying game e.g. 'soft' mouth or 'hard' mouth. |
| **Overreaching** | Fault in the trot caused by more angulation and drive from behind than in front, so that the rear feet are forced to step to one side of the forefeet to avoid interference or clipping. |
| **Pacing** | A lateral gait where the legs on the same side move in unison giving a rolling or rocking action of the body, (the normal gait is the diagonal supported gait in which the front and opposite rear legs move in unison). |
| **Paddling** | Front feet thrown sideways in loose manner often through 'tied' elbows. |
| **Pigmenation** | Natural colouring of skin and other tissue. |
| **Pinning** | Front feet pointing or turning inwards. |
| **Rangy** | Dog of slender build. |
| **Reachy** | With long neck. |
| **Set up** | Posed so as to make the most of the dog's appearance in the show ring. |
| **Stance** | Manner of standing |
| **Soundness** | The normal state of mental and physical well being. A term particularly applied to movement. |
| **Substance** | Solidity, with correct muscularity and condition. |
| **Throatiness** | An excess of loose skin in the throat area. |
| **Tied at Elbow** | Elbows set too close under the body, thus restricting movement. |
| **Weedy** | Light bone stucture, lacking substance. |

# INDEX

**A**

**B**
Back - 6, 41, 47-51
Balance - 12, 17
Bite - 12, 26-29
Bone - 12
Breed Standard - 12-13
   Development of - 90-92
   American - 92-95
Brisket - 6, 45

**C**
Carpus - 9
Character - 12, 19
Coat - 13, 72-75
Colour - 13, 74-77
Coupling - 12, 47
Croup - 6, 54-55, 60-61

**D**

**E**
Ears - 12, 21-25
Elbow - 6, 12, 34-35, 86-87,
Expression - 12, 21-25
Eyes - 12, 21-25

**F**
Faults - 13, 24, 70-71
Feet - 13, 66
Femur - 9
Fibula - 9
Forechest - 38, 24-25
Forelegs - 6, 12, 32-35
Forequarters - 12, 32-39

**G**
Gait - see movement

**H**
Head - 12, 21-25,
Height - 13, 68-69
Hips - 58-61, 86-87
Hindquarters - 13, 56-65

Hock - 6, 13, 56-59, 64-65, 86 - 87
Humerus - 9, 38-39

**I**
Index - 99

**J**
Jaws - 12, 26-29

**K**

**L**
Layback of shoulder - 36-39
Loin - 13, 47

**M**
Muscles - 11, 88-89
Mouth - 12, 26-29,
Movement - 13, 78-89
   Line of convergence 78
   Single tracking    80
   Moving close     80
   Rear Movement    81
   Front movement   82-83
   Side movement    84-85
   Anatomical sytems -
     Bones / Joints   86-87
     Muscles / Nerves  88 -89
Muzzle - 6, 12

**N**
Neck - 12, 31
Nervous system - 89
Nose - 12

**O**
Occiput - 6

**P**
Pastern - 6, 67
Patella - 9
Paw - 6
Pelvis - 9, 60-63
Phalanges - 9

**Q**

**R**
Radius - 9
Ribs - 9, 12, 40-47

**S**
Scapula - 9, 38-39,
Second Thigh - 6, 13, 62-63
Shoulder - 6, 12, 36-39, 86-87
Size - 13, 68-69
Skeleton - 9
Skull - 9, 12, 26-27
Spine - 41
Sternum - 9
Stifle - 6, 13, 62-63, 86-87
Stop - 6, 12

**T**
Tail - 6, 13, 41, 48, 52-55
Tarsus - 9,
Teeth - 12, 26-29
Temperament - 12, 21
Terminology - 96-98
Testicles - 13, 70
Thigh - 6
Topline, 13, 48-51
Tuck-up - 6, 45

**U**
Upper Arm - 6, 12, 36-39
Ulna - 9

**V**
Vertebrae - 9, 41

**W**
Weight - 68-69
Withers - 6
Working Ability -12, 15, 19
Wrist - 6, 86-87

**X**

**Y**

**Z**